BEGINNERS GUIDE To SELLING ON eBay 2024.

The art of a successful eBay selling.

Wilson Skylar

I0436316

CONTENTS

INTRODUCTION

Once upon a time, in a quiet town, there lived a young woman named Rahmmy. Rahmmy had a passion for vintage collectibles, and her apartment was adorned with treasures she had discovered in thrift stores and flea markets. One day, she stumbled upon a book titled "The Art of Successful eBay Selling" at a local bookstore. Intrigued, she decided to give it a read.As Rahmmy delved into the pages of the book, she discovered valuable insights into the world of online selling, particularly on eBay. The book covered topics ranging from creating compelling listings to understanding market trends and maximizing visibility. Rahmmy was inspired and decided to put the knowledge she gained into action.Armed with newfound wisdom, Rahmmy carefully curated her collection of vintage items and meticulously crafted eBay listings. She paid attention to the book's advice on using high-quality photos, writing detailed descriptions, and setting competitive prices. Rahmmy even incorporated some promotional strategies, offering limited-time discounts and bundling similar items to attract more buyers.

To her delight, Rahmmy's eBay venture started to gain traction. The vintage items she had once admired in her apartment were now finding new homes with eager buyers from across the country. Positive reviews began pouring in, praising Emma for her excellent packaging, accurate descriptions, and prompt shipping.Word spread quickly, and soon Rahmmy became known as a reputable seller in the online marketplace. Her eBay store flourished, and she started expanding her inventory to include not only vintage items but also handmade crafts and unique finds from her travels. Rahmmy's success wasn't just financial; it brought a sense of fulfillment and joy as she connected with people who shared her love for one-of-a-kind treasures.As Rahmmy continued to build her eBay empire, she often reflected on how a simple book had transformed her hobby into a thriving business. The Art of Successful eBay Selling had been more than just a guide—it had been the catalyst for a new chapter in Rahmmy's life.

Welcome to the dynamic world of eBay selling, where opportunities abound, and success is within your reach! Whether you're a seasoned e-commerce entrepreneur or just starting on your selling journey, this comprehensive guide is your go-to resource for navigating the intricacies of eBay and building a successful online business.

The Power of eBay: Why Sell Here?

eBay stands as a global e-commerce giant, offering a vibrant marketplace that connects buyers and sellers across the world. With millions of active users and an extensive range of product categories, eBay provides a unique platform for sellers to showcase their products, reach a diverse audience, and turn their passion into profit

CHAPTER 1:

Creating Your eBay Seller Account

The first step towards eBay success is creating a robust seller account. In this guide, we'll walk you through the process, from setting up your account details to understanding eBay's policies and best practices. Whether you're a casual seller or aiming for a full-fledged business, a well-crafted seller profile is the foundation for building trust and credibility with potential buyers.

Creating your eBay seller account is a straightforward process, and this step-by-step guide will walk you through each stage to ensure a smooth and successful setup.

Step one: Getting Started

Visit eBay's Homepage:

- Open your preferred web browser and go to www.ebay.com.
- Click on "Register":
- Locate the "Register" link at the top of the eBay homepage and click on it.

Step two: Account Type

- Choose "Create a Business Account" (Optional),depending on your selling goals, you can opt for a personal or business account.

Step three:Account Information:

- Enter Your Email Address,Provide a valid and regularly used email address.

- Create a Secure Password:
- Choose a strong password that combines letters, numbers, and symbols for security.

Step Four: Personal Information

- Enter Your Name:Provide your legal first and last name.
- Choose a User ID:Create a unique and memorable User ID. This will be your public identity on eBay.

Step Five Business Information (If Applicable)

- Enter Business Name (For Business Accounts):If you're setting up a business account, enter your business name.
- Business Contact Information:Provide business-specific contact details.

Step six:Create a PayPal Account

- Link a PayPal Account (Optional)Linking a PayPal account is recommended for smoother transactions.

Step seven:Review eBay's User Agreement and Privacy Policy

- Read and Accept Terms:Take the time to review eBay's User Agreement and Privacy Policy. Click on the checkbox to indicate that you accept these terms.

Step Eight:Confirmation Email

- Verify Your Email Address:eBay will send a confirmation email to the address you provided.

Congratulations! Your eBay Seller Account is Ready.Explore Your Seller DashboardOnce your account is confirmed, log in to your eBay account and explore your seller dashboard. Familiarize yourself with the various features and settings.

Setting Up Your Seller Profile

Creating a compelling seller profile on eBay is crucial for building trust with potential buyers and establishing credibility in the online marketplace. A well-crafted seller profile not only showcases your professionalism but also encourages buyers to choose your products over others. Follow this guide to ensure that your eBay seller profile stands out and attracts confident customers.

Step one:Access Your Seller Dashboard

- Log in to your eBay account and access your seller dashboard. Navigate to the "Account" or "Seller Hub" section, where you'll find options to manage your seller profile.

Step two:Update Personal Information

- Ensure that your personal information, such as your name and contact details, is accurate and up-to-date. This builds transparency and trust with potential buyers.

Step three:Profile Picture

- Consider adding a profile picture. While optional, a professional and friendly image of yourself can humanize your profile and create a personal connection with buyers.

Step Four: Business Information (For Business Accounts)

- If you have a business account, make sure your business name is displayed accurately. Provide relevant business contact information for smooth communication.

Step Five: User ID

- Your User ID is a key part of your identity on eBay. Ensure it is unique, easy to remember, and reflects a positive image. Avoid using personal information in your User ID for privacy reasons.

Step six: About Me Section

- Utilize the "About Me" section to share more about yourself or your business. This is an opportunity to highlight your expertise, your commitment to customer satisfaction, and any unique aspects that set you apart from other sellers.

Step seven: Feedback and Ratings

- Display your feedback score prominently. Positive feedback and high ratings provide reassurance to buyers. Address any negative feedback professionally and resolve issues promptly.

Step Eight:Customize Your Store

- If you have an eBay Store, customize it to create a branded experience for buyers. Choose a store theme, add a logo, and organize your products into categories for easy navigation.

Step nine:Payment and Return Policies

- Clearly state your accepted payment methods and return policies. Transparent policies contribute to a positive buyer experience and can increase trust in your seller profile.

step Ten: Regularly Update Your Profile:

- Keep your seller profile dynamic and relevant. Regularly update information, such as business hours, if applicable, and any changes to your contact details.

Step Eleven:Professional Communication:

- Respond promptly and professionally to buyer inquiries. Positive communication contributes to positive feedback and enhances your seller reputation.

By investing time in setting up a comprehensive and appealing seller profile, you lay the foundation for a successful eBay selling experience. A well-crafted profile not only instills confidence in buyers but also positions you as a reliable and trustworthy seller in the competitive world of online commerce.

Account Verification and Security on eBay

Ensuring the security of your eBay account is paramount for a successful and trustworthy selling experience. Account verification and robust security measures protect your personal information, financial details, and reputation as a seller. Follow this comprehensive guide to fortify the security of your eBay account.

1. Two-Step Verification:

- Enable two-step verification for an additional layer of security. This typically involves receiving a verification code on your mobile device or email when logging in.

2. Secure Password Practices

Use a strong and unique password for your eBay account. Incorporate a combination of uppercase and lowercase letters, numbers, and symbols. Avoid easily guessable information, such as birthdays or common words.

- Change your password periodically and refrain from using the same password across multiple platforms.

3. Account Verification:

- eBay may request additional verification to ensure the security of your account. This could include confirming your identity through documents or additional information.
- If prompted, follow the instructions provided by eBay to complete the verification process promptly.

4. Regularly Review Account Activity:

- Periodically review your account activity to identify any unauthorized or suspicious transactions. eBay provides a detailed account activity log that includes purchases, bids, and changes to your account settings.

5. Secure Your Email Address:

- Your email address is closely tied to your eBay account. Secure it with a strong password and enable two-step verification if your email provider supports it.
- Avoid clicking on suspicious links or downloading attachments from unknown sources in your email, as phishing attempts often target email accounts.

6. Stay Informed About Security Alerts:

- Keep an eye on security alerts and updates from eBay. Stay informed about any potential threats, scams, or security vulnerabilities that may affect your account.

7. Beware of Phishing Attempts:

- Be cautious of phishing emails or messages that appear to be from eBay. eBay will never ask you to provide sensitive information, such as passwords or credit card details, through email.
- Verify the authenticity of messages by checking your eBay messages directly through your account rather than clicking on links in emails.

8. Secure Payment Methods:

- If you link a PayPal account or other payment method to your eBay account, ensure that these accounts also have strong security measures in place. Regularly review transactions for any discrepancies.

9. Logout After Each Session:

- Always log out of your eBay account after each session, especially if using a public or shared computer. This prevents unauthorized access to your account.

10. Keep Software and Devices Updated:

- Regularly update your computer, smartphone, and any devices used for accessing eBay. Software updates often include security patches that protect against vulnerabilities.

By following these steps and remaining vigilant, you contribute to the overall security of your eBay account. A secure account not only protects your personal information but also ensures a positive and trustworthy experience for both buyers and sellers on the eBay platform.

Chapter 2:

Crafting Irresistible Listings

The art of selling on eBay begins with creating compelling listings. Learn how to optimize your product titles, write engaging descriptions, and showcase your items with captivating images. We'll explore strategies for pricing your products competitively and leveraging eBay's listing features to maximize visibility and attract eager buyers

Optimizing Product Titles on eBay

Crafting compelling and optimized product titles is a critical aspect of selling on eBay. A well-optimized title not only enhances the visibility of your listings in search results but also entices potential buyers to click and explore further. Follow this comprehensive guide to master the art of optimizing your product titles on eBay.

Clarity and Relevance:

Start with a clear and concise product name that accurately describes the item you're selling.Ensure that the title is relevant to the product and matches the terms buyers are likely to search for.

Include Key Product Details:

Incorporate essential details such as brand, model, size, color, and other relevant specifications directly into the title.

Keyword Research:

Conduct thorough keyword research to identify terms that potential buyers commonly use when searching for products similar to yours.Use eBay's search bar to see suggested search terms related to your product.

Prioritize Important Information:

Place the most critical information at the beginning of the title. Buyers often skim through search results, so make sure key details are prominent.

Avoid Keyword Stuffing:

While including keywords is crucial, avoid overloading your title with excessive keywords. Maintain a balance to ensure readability and relevance.

Use Standard Spelling and Avoid Special Characters:

Use proper spelling and avoid unnecessary special characters in your titles. This ensures that your listings are easily readable and understood by both buyers and search algorithms.

Capitalization and Formatting:

Use capitalization to highlight important words in your title. Avoid writing the entire title in uppercase, as it can be perceived as spammy.

Check Character Limit:

eBay has a character limit for product titles. Be concise and make every character count. Ensure that the most critical information is within the first 80-100 characters.

Localize for Global Buyers:

If you are selling internationally, consider including regional terms and language variations to attract a broader audience.

Stay Compliant with eBay Policies:

Familiarize yourself with eBay's policies regarding product titles. Avoid misleading information, symbols, or excessive capitalization that could lead to penalties.

By implementing these strategies, you'll enhance the visibility of your listings and increase the likelihood of attracting potential buyers. Optimized product titles contribute significantly to your success on eBay by improving search rankings and ultimately driving more sales.

Crafting Engaging Item Descriptions

The item description is your canvas for painting a vivid picture of your product and persuading potential buyers to make a purchase. An engaging and informative description not only instills confidence in your buyers but also sets your listing apart in the competitive landscape of eBay. Follow this comprehensive guide to master the art of crafting compelling item descriptions that captivate your audience.

1. Start with a Clear and Concise Introduction:

Begin your item description with a concise introduction that summarizes the key features and benefits of the product.

2. Highlight Key Features:

Identify the standout features of your product and highlight them in a dedicated section. Bullet points work well for easy readability.

3. Provide Technical Specifications:

Include relevant technical details such as dimensions, materials, weight, and any other specifications that buyers might consider when making a purchase.

4. Use High-Quality Images:

Supplement your description with high-quality images that showcase the product from various aangles.Add captions to your images to reinforce key points in the description.

5. Address Potential Concerns:

Anticipate and address potential concerns or questions buyers might have. This could include details about warranty, return policy, or compatibility with other products.

6. Tell a Story:

Weave a narrative around your product. Describe how it can be used or share a scenario where it would be particularly useful.

7. Use Descriptive Language:

Choose words that evoke emotions and clearly communicate the benefits of your product. Use adjectives that paint a vivid picture.e.g "plush and inviting sofa for cozy evenings."

8. Encourage Questions and Engagement:

Invite buyers to ask questions or seek clarification. This engagement not only helps buyers but also signals to eBay that your listing is active and responsive.

9. Proofread and Edit:

Ensure your description is free of spelling and grammatical errors. Proofread your content before publishing.

Showcasing products with high quality images

Creating a visually appealing product showcase with high-quality images is crucial for attracting customers and making a positive impression. Here are some tips on how to showcase products effectively using high-quality images:

1. Use Professional Photography:

- Invest in a professional photographer or learn photography techniques to capture your products in the best light.
- Ensure proper lighting, focus, and composition for each shot.

2. Highlight Key Features:

- Showcase important features and details of the product. Capture shots from different angles to provide a comprehensive view.
- Use close-ups to highlight intricate details.

3. Consistent Backgrounds:

- Maintain consistency in the background to create a cohesive look across your product images.

- Consider using a plain, neutral background that doesn't distract from the product.

4. Multiple Angles:

- Include images from various angles to give customers a complete understanding of the product's appearance.
- Display the product in use to help customers visualize its real-world application.

5. High Resolution:

- Ensure that images are of high resolution to allow customers to zoom in and examine details.
- High-resolution images convey a sense of professionalism and quality.

6. Use Props Wisely:

- Consider using props that complement the product and provide context without overshadowing it.
- Props can help customers envision how the product fits into their lives.

7. Consistent Branding:

- Maintain a consistent style and branding across all product images.
- Use a similar color palette, font, and style to reinforce your brand identity.

8. Image Editing:

- Use photo editing tools to enhance images, adjust colors, and correct any imperfections.
- Be careful not to over-edit, as authenticity is crucial.

9. Showcase Variations:

- If your product comes in different colors, sizes, or styles, showcase each variation separately.
- Provide clear labeling or categorization for easy navigation.

10. Responsive Design:

- Optimize images for various devices and screen sizes to ensure a seamless viewing experience.
- Consider implementing a responsive image gallery on your website.

11. Create a Story:

- Arrange images in a way that tells a story about the product.
- Start with an attention-grabbing image and follow with images that highlight different aspects.

12. Testimonials and Reviews:

- Integrate customer testimonials or reviews with images to build trust and credibility.
- Consider including before-and-after images if applicable.

13. Social Media Integration:

- Share your high-quality images on social media platforms to reach a wider audience.
- Use platforms like Instagram and Pinterest, known for their visual focus.

The goal is to provide potential customers with a comprehensive understanding of your product through visually appealing and high-quality images. It's an investment that can significantly impact the perception of your brand and drive sales.

Chapter 3:

Navigating eBay Tools and Features.

In the ever-evolving realm of online commerce, eBay has established itself as a global marketplace, offering a platform where sellers can connect with a vast audience.To thrive in this dynamic marketplace, understanding and effectively utilizing eBay's diverse array of tools and features is key. Whether you're a seasoned seller or just dipping your toes into online commerce, this guide is your roadmap to navigating the robust tools and features that eBay has to offer. From streamlining your listings to harnessing powerful analytics, this introduction will set the stage for your journey towards eBay mastery. Let's delve into the tools and features that will elevate your selling experience and help you carve out success in the competitive world of online retail.

The Power of eBay Promoted Listings

In the bustling marketplace of eBay, standing out is crucial for success, and eBay's Promoted Listings feature is your secret weapon for boosting visibility. This powerful tool allows sellers to enhance the discoverability of their products by strategically placing them at the forefront of search results.

How It Works:

- Select Listings: Choose the products you want to promote.
- Set Ad Rates: Determine the percentage fee you're willing to pay for each sale generated through the Promoted Listings.
- Monitor Performance: Keep a close eye on the performance analytics provided by eBay.

Benefits:

- Increased Visibility: Stand out in a crowded marketplace by ensuring your products appear prominently in search results.
- Cost-Effective Advertising: Sellers have control over advertising costs with the ability to set their own ad rates.
- Data-Driven Decisions: Leverage performance analytics to make informed decisions, refining your strategy for better results.

In the competitive world of online retail, eBay Promoted Listings give sellers a powerful edge. By strategically showcasing your products to a broader audience, you not only increase visibility but also enhance the likelihood of converting searches into successful sales.

Elevate your eBay selling experience with Promoted Listings and unlock the full potential of your online business.

Skyrocket Your Sales: Effective Seller Promotions on eBay

In the dynamic world of e-commerce, standing out from the crowd is essential for sellers looking to boost sales and attract a broader customer base. eBay provides a robust platform for sellers to create enticing promotions, offering a strategic advantage in a competitive marketplace. Let's explore how you can leverage seller promotions to supercharge your sales:

1. Types of Seller Promotions:

- Percentage Off Deals
- BOGO (Buy One, Get One) Offers
- Order Size Discounts
- Free Shipping Promotions

2. Strategic Timing:

- Flash Sales
- Holiday and Seasonal Promotions

3. Clear Communication:

- Promotional Banners
- Customized Listing Titles

4. Discount Coupons:

- Exclusive Discounts
- Time-Limited Coupons

6. Leverage eBay Tools:

- Promoted Listings
- Markdown Manager

7. Monitor and Analyze:

- Performance Metrics

- Buyer Behaviour

Seller promotions on eBay are a dynamic and powerful tool for increasing sales, attracting new customers, and retaining existing ones. By strategically designing and implementing enticing promotions, sellers can create a compelling shopping experience that not only meets but exceeds buyer expectations. Stay ahead of the competition and boost your sales with well-crafted seller promotions tailored to your target audience and business goals.

Advanced stragegies for seasoned sellers

As a seasoned seller on eBay, the journey to sustained success involves not just mastering the basics but also implementing advanced strategies that set you apart in a competitive e-commerce landscape. In this guide, we'll explore a range of advanced tactics that seasoned sellers can leverage to optimize their operations, maximize profits, and stay ahead of the curve.

1. Dynamic Pricing Optimization:

- *Competitive Analysis:* Regularly analyze competitor pricing and adjust your own dynamically to remain competitive while maintaining profitability.
- *Automated Tools:* Implement automated pricing tools that take into account market conditions, competitor pricing, and other variables to optimize your pricing strategy.

2. Strategic Inventory Management:

- *Demand Forecasting:* Use data analytics and historical sales data to forecast demand accurately. .

- *Seasonal Adjustments:* Adjust inventory levels strategically to align with seasonal demand fluctuations, ensuring optimal stock levels during peak periods.

3. Cross-Promotion and Upselling:

- *Bundle Offers:* Create enticing bundle offers to encourage customers to purchase complementary products together, increasing the average order value.
- *Upselling Techniques:* Implement strategic upselling by showcasing premium or upgraded items to enhance customer transactions.

4. Optimized Product Listings:

- *Keyword Optimization:* Conduct thorough keyword research and strategically incorporate high-performing keywords into product titles and descriptions for improved search visibility.
- *Enhanced Content:* Utilize eBay's enhanced content features to provide a richer and more informative shopping experience.

5. Personalized Customer Engagement:

- *Customer Segmentation:* Segment your customer base based on purchasing behavior, preferences, and demographics. Tailor marketing and communication strategies for each segment.
- *Email Marketing Automation:* Implement automated email marketing campaigns, including personalized product recommendations, exclusive offers, and targeted promotions.

6.Brand Building and Store Customization:

- *Branding:* Establish a strong brand presence by customizing your eBay store. Consistent branding fosters trust and loyalty among buyers.
- *HTML and CSS Customization:* Use HTML and CSS to customize your store layout, creating a visually appealing and unique storefront.

7. Continuous Learning and Adaptation:

- *Stay Informed:* Regularly update your knowledge on eBay policies, algorithms, and industry trends by attending webinars, conferences, and industry events.
- *Adaptability:* Maintain an adaptable mindset, experimenting with new strategies and technologies to stay ahead of evolving market dynamics.

In the dynamic world of e-commerce, seasoned sellers must continually refine and innovate their strategies to remain at the forefront. By incorporating these advanced tactics into your approach, you not only enhance your competitive edge but also position yourself for sustained success on eBay. **The key lies in a commitment to continuous improvement and an ability to adapt to the ever-changing landscape of online retail.**

Chapter 4:

Effective store management

In the dynamic realm of e-commerce, the success of an online store is not only determined by the quality of products but also by the effectiveness of its management. Effective store management is the linchpin of a successful e-commerce venture, encompassing a holistic approach to various business facets. From strategic inventory management and personalized customer engagement to optimized product listings and efficient order fulfillment, it involves meticulous planning and execution. Marketing strategies, data-driven decision-making, and the integration of technology play pivotal roles, fostering visibility and enhancing the overall shopping experience. Financial oversight, adaptability to market trends, and a commitment to continuous improvement complete the picture. By embracing these principles, businesses can navigate the complexities of online retail, fostering growth, customer satisfaction, and long-term success.

Organizing Your Inventory for Business Success

Effectively organizing your inventory is a cornerstone of efficient business operations, ensuring that products are readily accessible, order fulfillment is streamlined, and customer satisfaction is optimized. Here's a guide to mastering the art of inventory organization:

1. Categorization and Segmentation:

- *Group Similar Items:* Categorize products based on similarities in type, size, or usage to streamline storage and retrieval processes.
- *ABC Analysis:* Prioritize items based on sales frequency to allocate storage space accordingly—high-selling items in easily accessible areas.

2. Strategic Storage Systems:

- *Utilize Shelving and Racking:* Invest in shelving and racking systems to maximize vertical space, ensuring an organized and easily navigable storage environment.
- *Bin and Drawer Systems:* Employ bins, drawers, or labeled containers for smaller items, minimizing the risk of misplacement.

3. Clear Identification and Labeling:

- *Barcoding and RFID:* Implement barcode or RFID systems for accurate tracking and swift identification of items during inventory checks.
- *Clearly Labeled Shelves:* Ensure shelves and storage bins are clearly labeled, facilitating quick and error-free picking.

4. First-In-First-Out (FIFO) System:

- *Rotation Strategy:* Adopt the FIFO system to minimize product spoilage or obsolescence by using older stock first.
- *Expiry Date Tracking:* Clearly mark and monitor products with expiration dates, if applicable, to avoid selling expired goods.

5. Regular Audits and Cycle Counts:

- *Scheduled Audits:* Conduct regular inventory audits to reconcile physical stock with recorded levels and identify discrepancies promptly.
- *Cycle Counts:* Implement cycle counting, focusing on specific product categories at different intervals, reducing disruptions in daily operations.

6. Supplier Collaboration:

- *Communication Channels:* Maintain open lines of communication with suppliers to streamline restocking processes, negotiate favorable terms, and stay informed about product availability.
- *Vendor-Managed Inventory (VMI):* Explore VMI agreements with key suppliers, allowing them to manage your inventory levels based on pre-established criteria.

7.. Employee Training and Accountability:

- *Training Programs:* Provide comprehensive training for staff on inventory management procedures, emphasizing accuracy and efficiency.
- *Accountability Measures:* Implement accountability measures to ensure that employees adhere to established protocols, minimizing errors and discrepancies.

8. Adaptability and Continuous Improvement:

- *Feedback Mechanisms:* Solicit feedback from employees involved in inventory management to identify bottlenecks and areas for improvement.
- *Adapt to Changing Needs:* Stay adaptable to changes in product lines, market demands, and business growth, adjusting inventory management strategies accordingly.

By implementing these organizational strategies, businesses can maintain a well-ordered inventory, ensuring smoother operations, reducing costs, and ultimately enhancing customer satisfaction through timely and accurate order fulfillment.

Providing Excellent customer service on eBay

Providing excellent customer service on eBay is crucial for building trust, attracting repeat business, and maintaining a positive seller reputation. Here are some tips to ensure you deliver exceptional customer service on the eBay platform:

1.Clear and Accurate Item Descriptions:

- Provide detailed and accurate descriptions of your items. Include information about the product's features, condition, and any relevant specifications.

2. High-Quality Images:

- Include clear, high-resolution images of your products from various angles. This helps buyers get a better understanding of the item's condition and appearance.

3. Prompt Communication:

- Respond to buyer inquiries and messages promptly. Address any questions or concerns they may have and provide helpful, friendly, and professional responses.

4. Fast Shipping:

- Ship items promptly after receiving payment. Fast and reliable shipping enhances the overall customer experience.

5. Secure Packaging:

- Pack items securely to prevent damage during transit. Proper packaging not only protects the item but also demonstrates your commitment to delivering quality products to your customers.

6. Offer Special Deals and Promotions:

- Consider offering special deals or promotions, such as discounted shipping on multiple items or limited-time sales.

7. Regularly Update Your eBay Store:

○ Keep your eBay store updated with new products, promotions, and relevant information. An active and well-maintained store can attract more customers and showcase your commitment to your eBay business.

8. Educate Buyers:

○ Provide information and guides related to your products. Educated buyers are often more satisfied, and it reduces the likelihood of misunderstandings or dissatisfaction.

By consistently providing excellent customer service on eBay, you not only enhance the buying experience for your customers but also contribute to the long-term success and growth of your online business.

Building And Maintaining Positive Seller Reputation

Building and maintaining a positive seller reputation online is essential. Provide accurate product descriptions, high-quality images, and competitive pricing for transparency. Prioritize prompt communication, fast shipping, and secure packaging to showcase professionalism. Encourage positive reviews from satisfied customers to build credibility. Maintain consistency in product quality, customer service, and shipping practices. Handle customer issues promptly and professionally to turn challenges into positive experiences. Clearly outline return and refund policies to manage customer expectations.

Stay informed about platform policies and adapt practices accordingly. Regularly update product listings and remove unavailable items to prevent negative experiences. Proactively address customer concerns and seek ways to improve products and services based on feedback. Embrace a customer-centric approach to foster trust and credibility.

Chapter 5:

Understanding eBay Fees

Understanding eBay fees is crucial for sellers to effectively manage their costs and maximize profitability. eBay charges sellers various fees, including an insertion fee for listing an item, final value fees based on the item's sale price, and additional fees for optional listing upgrades. Sellers should be aware of the fee structure, which can vary based on the type of item, format, and seller level. Consider factors like shipping costs and payment method fees, as they also impact overall expenses. Regularly review eBay's fee policies and use the fee calculator to estimate costs accurately. By understanding and carefully managing fees, sellers can optimize their pricing strategies and enhance their overall eBay selling experience.

Demystifying eBay's Fee Structure

Demystifying eBay's fee structure is critical for sellers to effectively manage their expenses and maximize profits. eBay employs a comprehensive fee system that includes various charges, and understanding these intricacies is key to navigating the platform successfully. Here's a breakdown of eBay's fee structure:

1. Insertion Fees:

- eBay charges an insertion fee for listing an item. This fee is based on the type of listing (auction-style or fixed price), the category of the item, and any optional listing upgrades.

2. Final Value Fees (FVF):

- The final value fee is a percentage of the total amount a buyer pays for an item, including shipping and handling.

3. Optional Listing Upgrades:

- ○ Sellers can choose optional upgrades for their listings, such as adding subtitles, extra photos, or highlighting the listing. Each of these upgrades incurs an additional fee, and sellers need to weigh the benefits against the costs.

4. Promoted Listings:

- ○ Sellers can opt for promoted listings to increase the visibility of their products.

5. Shipping Costs and Impact on Fees:

- ○ Shipping costs are a crucial component of eBay fees. Final value fees are assessed on the total amount the buyer pays, including shipping. Sellers need to factor this into their pricing strategy to ensure they cover expenses and maintain profitability.

6. Payment Processing Fees:

- ○ eBay manages payments for many sellers, and payment processing fees are applied to the transaction amount, including the item price, shipping, and any sales tax.

7. Fee Calculators:

- ○ eBay provides fee calculators that allow sellers to estimate their fees based on various scenarios. These tools are valuable for planning and setting competitive prices.

8. Stay Informed about Policy Changes:

- ○ eBay occasionally updates its fee structure and policies. Sellers should stay informed about any changes through official communications and updates from eBay.

Pricing strategies for profitability

Demystifying eBay's fee structure empowers sellers to make informed decisions about their pricing, listing strategies, and overall financial management. Regularly reviewing and optimizing these strategies ensures that sellers can navigate the platform successfully and maximize their profitability.

Implementing effective pricing strategies is crucial for maximizing profitability in business. Here are key considerations and strategies to optimize pricing for increased profitability:

1. Cost-Plus Pricing:
   - Determine the total cost of producing or acquiring a product, then add a markup to establish the selling price.

2. Competitive Pricing:
   - Analyze competitors' pricing for similar products and position your prices competitively.

3. Value-Based Pricing:
   - Set prices based on the perceived value of your product or service in the eyes of customers.

4. Dynamic Pricing:
   - Adjust prices in real-time based on market demand, seasonality, or other relevant factors. This strategy allows for flexibility and responsiveness to changing market conditions.

5. Subscription and Tiered Pricing:
   - Introduce subscription models or tiered pricing structures to encourage customer loyalty and provide options for different customer segments with varying needs and budgets.

6. Geographic Pricing:

- Consider adjusting prices based on geographic locations, accounting for regional differences in purchasing power and market conditions..

7. Limited-Time Offers:

- Introduce scarcity by offering limited-time promotions or exclusive deals. This can create a sense of urgency and drive quicker purchasing decisions.

8.Relationship-Based Pricing:

- Offer special pricing or loyalty programs for repeat customers. Building long-term relationships can lead to a more stable and profitable customer base.

9.Collaborative Pricing with Suppliers:

- Negotiate favorable terms with suppliers to lower input costs, contributing to higher profit margins without necessarily increasing prices for customers.

Effective pricing strategies involve a combination of these approaches, tailored to the specific business, industry, and target audience. Regularly evaluate and adapt pricing strategies to ensure ongoing profitability and competitivenes

Chapter 6:

Strategies of Growth

eBay focuses on growth through global expansion, technological innovation, and strategic partnerships. Diversification of product offerings and a strong mobile presence contribute to an enhanced marketplace. Seller empowerment, AI-driven personalization, and buyer loyalty programs drive increased engagement. Streamlined checkout processes and sustainability initiatives further boost customer satisfaction and appeal. These combined strategies position eBay as a competitive and evolving platform in the dynamic e-commerce landscape.

Marketing your eBay store

Effectively marketing your eBay store is crucial for increasing visibility, attracting customers, and driving sales. Here are key strategies for promoting your eBay store:

1. ## Optimized eBay Listings:
   - Craft compelling, keyword-rich titles and detailed product descriptions to improve search visibility within eBay. Utilize high-quality images to showcase your products.

2. **Utilize eBay Promotions:**
   - Leverage eBay's promotional tools, such as sales and discounts, to attract buyers.

3. ## eBay Store Subscription:
   - Consider subscribing to an eBay store, which provides additional marketing tools, customization options, and discounted fees.

4. Cross-Promotion:

○ Cross-promote related items within your store to encourage customers to explore additional products, increasing the likelihood of multiple purchases.

5. Social Media Marketing:

○ Share your eBay store and product listings on social media platforms. Utilize Facebook, Instagram, Twitter, and other channels to reach a broader audience.

6. Email Marketing:

○ Build and maintain an email list of customers who have opted in to receive updates.

7. Paid Advertising:

○ Utilize eBay's sponsored listings feature for paid advertising. This can increase the visibility of your products in search results and attract more potential customers.

8. Optimize for Mobile Users:

○ Ensure that your eBay store is mobile-friendly, as a significant portion of users accesses the platform through smartphones. A responsive design enhances the user experience.

9. Implement SEO Best Practices:

○ Apply search engine optimization (SEO) best practices within your eBay store, using relevant keywords in titles, descriptions, and other fields to improve discoverability.

10. Run Limited-Time Promotions:

○ Create a sense of urgency by running limited-time promotions or flash sales. This can encourage quicker decision-making among potential buyers.

By implementing a combination of these strategies, you can effectively market your eBay store, increase visibility, and attract a broader audience of potential customers. Regularly evaluate the performance of your marketing efforts and adjust strategies based on customer behavior and market trends.

Social media integration for Increased reach

Integrating social media into your marketing strategy is a powerful way to increase the reach of your eBay store and connect with a wider audience. Here are key strategies for effective social media integration:

1. Choose Relevant Platforms:
  - Identify the social media platforms that align with your target audience and product niche. Common platforms include Facebook, Instagram, Twitter, Pinterest, and LinkedIn.

2. Create a Consistent Brand Presence:
  - Maintain a cohesive brand presence across your eBay store and social media profiles. Use consistent branding elements, such as logos, colors, and messaging, to enhance brand recognition.

3. Share Compelling Content:
  - Regularly share engaging content, including product images, promotions, and behind-the-scenes glimpses. Diversify content to include videos, customer testimonials, and relevant industry news.

4. Engage with Your Audience:
  - Actively engage with your social media audience by responding to comments, messages, and mentions.

5. Host Contests and Giveaways:
  - Organize contests or giveaways on social media platforms to encourage user participation, increase brand visibility, and attract new followers.

6.Share User-Generated Content:

- Encourage customers to share their experiences with your products and repost user-generated content. This builds authenticity and trust while expanding your content reach.

6. Promote Limited-Time Offers:

- Create a sense of urgency by promoting limited-time offers or exclusive deals on social media. This can drive traffic to your eBay store and boost sales.

7. Optimize Posting Times:

- Analyze the peak engagement times for your audience on different social media platforms and schedule posts accordingly.

8. Use Social Media Analytics:

- Utilize analytics tools provided by social media platforms to track the performance of your posts, understand audience behavior, and refine your strategy for maximum impact.

By integrating these strategies, you can effectively leverage social media to increase the reach of your eBay store, engage with potential customers, and drive sales. Regularly assess the performance of your social media efforts and adjust your approach based on evolving trends and audience preferences.

Adapting to market trends and changes

Adapting to market trends and changes is essential for businesses to remain relevant and thrive in a dynamic environment. Here are key strategies for successfully navigating shifts in market dynamics:

1.Continuous Monitoring:

Regularly monitor industry trends, consumer behavior, and competitive landscapes to stay informed about changes affecting your market.

2.Flexibility and Agility:

Cultivate a culture of flexibility within your organization. Be prepared to pivot strategies quickly in response to emerging trends or unexpected market shifts.

3.Customer Feedback and Data Analysis:

Actively seek customer feedback and utilize data analytics to understand customer preferences.

4.Innovation and R&D:

Invest in research and development to foster innovation. Stay ahead of the curve by introducing new products or services that align with evolving market demands.

5.Adaptive Marketing Strategies:

Adjust marketing strategies in response to changing consumer behaviors and preferences.

6.Employee Training and Development:

Ensure that your workforce is equipped with the skills needed to adapt to technological advancements and changing market dynamics. Continuous training fosters adaptability.

7.Risk Management:

Develop robust risk management strategies to identify and mitigate potential challenges arising from market fluctuations, economic shifts, or unforeseen circumstances.

8.Scenario Planning:

Conduct scenario planning exercises to anticipate potential market shifts and develop strategies to address various future scenarios.

9.Regular Business Assessments:

Conduct regular assessments of your business performance and strategies. This allows for timely adjustments to align with market changes and emerging opportunities.

By adopting a proactive and adaptive mindset, businesses can position themselves to thrive in an ever-changing marketplace. The ability to recognize and respond to market trends ensures resilience and long-term success.

Frequently Asked Questions (FAQ)

1. How do I create an eBay account?
   - To create an eBay account, visit the eBay website and click on the "Register" or "Sign Up" option. Follow the prompts to provide necessary information such as your email address, name, and password.
2. What items are not allowed to be sold on eBay?
   - eBay prohibits the sale of certain items, including illegal items, prescription drugs, firearms, and certain types of adult content. Refer to eBay's prohibited and restricted items policy for a comprehensive list.
3. How can I list an item for sale on eBay?
   - To list an item, log in to your eBay account, click on "Sell" at the top of the page, and follow the step-by-step process to create a listing. Provide accurate details about your item, set a price, and choose your preferred shipping options.
4. What are eBay fees and how are they calculated?
   - eBay charges fees for listing items and a final value fee based on the sale price. The exact fees depend on factors like the type of listing, category, and any optional upgrades. eBay provides a fee calculator for sellers to estimate costs.
5. How does eBay's bidding system work?
   - eBay uses a bidding system for auction-style listings. Buyers place bids on items, and the highest bidder at the end of the auction wins. Alternatively, sellers can choose to list items with a fixed price (Buy It Now) without bidding.
6. Can I cancel a bid on eBay?

- In general, bids on eBay are considered binding contracts, and canceling a bid is discouraged. However, there are specific situations, such as a bidder making a mistake, where eBay allows bid retractions. Sellers can also cancel bids under certain circumstances.

7. How can I protect myself from scams on eBay?

- To protect yourself, use secure payment methods, be cautious of suspicious emails or messages, and carefully review a seller's feedback and ratings. eBay's Buyer Protection program offers additional safeguards for eligible purchases.

8. What is the eBay Global Shipping Program?

- The Global Shipping Program allows sellers to ship items internationally while eBay handles customs and import duties. Buyers from eligible countries can purchase items with international shipping through this program.

9. How can I improve my seller rating on eBay?

- To improve your seller rating, provide accurate item descriptions, ship items promptly, communicate effectively with buyers, and resolve any issues professionally. Positive feedback from satisfied customers contributes to a higher rating.

10. Can I change or upgrade my eBay store subscription?

- Yes, sellers can change or upgrade their eBay store subscription at any time. Navigate to the "Subscription" section in the Seller Hub to make adjustments based on your business needs.

Remember to refer to eBay's official help and support resources for the most accurate and up-to-date information regarding frequently asked questions